A Day at the Snack Stand

ISBN 13: 978-0-15-360494-2
ISBN 10: 0-15-360494-8

1 2 3 4 5 6 7 8 9 10 039 16 15 14 13 12 11 10 09 08 07

A Day at the Snack Stand

by Sarah Mastrianni

Photographs by Patrick Espinosa

Harcourt
SCHOOL PUBLISHERS

Chapter 1:
Oak Grove Park

The children in Oak Grove like to play soccer. Soccer teams practice during the week. Teams play games on Saturday. Many fans watch games at the park. They cheer. Everyone has fun.

There is a snack stand at the park. Players and fans can buy food and drinks. There are many healthful choices at the stand. The snacks give players energy. Cold drinks taste good to thirsty players.

Volunteers help at the snack stand.
Today the Lee family will work at the stand.
The Lees will work together. Each of them
will have a job. The snack stand is a busy
place on game days.

The Lees are excited about working. They talk about the jobs they will do. Mr. and Mrs. Lee will set up the snack stand. Sue and Jade will take orders. The Lees can hardly wait to get started.

Chapter 2:
Getting the Snack Stand Ready for Customers

Mrs. Lee arrives at the snack stand. She will help get food and drinks ready. People will arrive for the games soon.

Mrs. Lee wants people to see the snacks for sale. She will place juice boxes at each customer window. She will put granola bars at the windows, too.

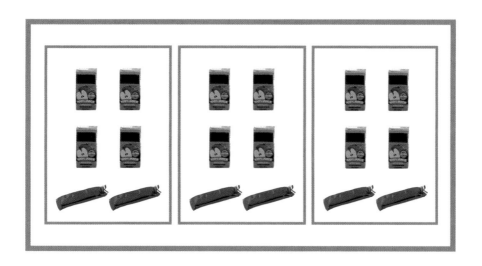

Mrs. Lee has 12 juice boxes. She divides 12 juice boxes into 3 equal groups. Each group has 4 juice boxes in it.

Mrs. Lee has 6 granola bars. She divides the 6 bars into groups of 2.

She places juice at each window. Then, she places granola bars at each window.

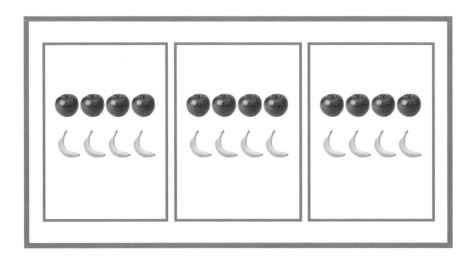

Mrs. Lee gets some fruit. She has apples and bananas. She divides the apples into 3 equal groups. Each group has 4 apples in it. Then, she divides 12 bananas into 3 equal groups. Mrs. Lee puts 4 apples and 4 bananas at each window.

Mr. Lee arrives at the snack stand. He opens the refrigerator. He sees many bottles of water. Mr. Lee needs to count the bottles on each shelf. He needs to keep track of the number of bottles they sell today.

Mr. Lee counts the bottles of water. There are 4 rows of bottles on each shelf. Each row has 7 bottles in it. Mr. Lee multiplies the number of bottles in each row by the number of rows.

He finds the total number of bottles on each shelf.

$4 \times 7 = 28$

There are 28 bottles on each shelf. There are 5 shelves. He adds.

```
    4
   28
   28
   28
   28
 + 28
 ─────
  140
```

The Lees have 140 bottles of water to sell.

Chapter 3:
Soccer Makes
Everyone Hungry!

Jade and Sue help, too. They work together at a window. Sue takes orders from customers. Then, she fills the orders. Jade takes the money from customers. Then, she gives them change. Sue and Jade make a good team.

Mrs. Todd comes to the window. Sue and Jade greet her. Sue asks Mrs. Todd if she can take her order. Mrs. Todd orders an apple. She orders a bagel, too.

apple	$0.50	
bagel	$0.75	

The apple costs $0.50. The bagel costs $0.75.

Sue adds.

Mrs. Todd's Order		
apple	(two quarters)	$0.50
bagel	(three quarters)	+ $0.75
		$1.25

Mrs. Todd's order costs $1.25. She gives Jade $2.00. Jade subtracts to find Mrs. Todd's change.

$2.00
− $1.25
$0.75

Mrs. Todd will get $0.75 in change. Jade hands her the coins. Sue gives Mrs. Todd her food. Mrs. Todd thanks them.

Beth is Jade's friend. She and her Dad are next in line. Beth says hello to Sue and Jade. Her game is over. She scored two goals. Her team won the game. Beth is happy.

Beth is hungry for a snack. She thinks about what she would like to eat. She orders a sandwich. She orders water, too.

sandwich	$2.35	
water	$1.75	

The sandwich costs $2.35. The water costs $1.75.

Sue adds.

Beth's Order		
sandwich		$\begin{array}{r} \text{I I} \\ \$2.35 \\ + \$1.75 \\ \hline \$4.10 \end{array}$
water		

Beth's order costs $4.10. Beth gives Jade a five-dollar bill. Jade subtracts to find Beth's change.

$$\begin{array}{r} \overset{4\ 10}{\$\cancel{5}.\cancel{0}0} \\ - \$4.10 \\ \hline \$0.90 \end{array}$$

Jade gives Beth $0.90 in change. Sue hands Beth her order. Beth walks over to a picnic table to eat her snack.

Chapter 4:
Everyone is a Winner

It is late in the day. The soccer games are ending. People begin to leave the park. The Lee family cleans the snack stand. They put everything away. Mrs. Lee counts the money. There is one more thing to do.

Mr. Lee opens the refrigerator to count the drinks. He needs to order more water. People will need plenty of water for next Saturday. Mr. Lee thinks. How many bottles of water did they have when they opened the snack stand? How many bottles are left?

The Lees began the day with 140 bottles of water. There are 22 bottles of water left. Mr. Lee subtracts.

$$\begin{array}{r} \overset{3\ 10}{1\cancel{4}\cancel{0}} \\ -\ 22 \\ \hline 118 \end{array}$$

Mr. Lee will order 118 bottles of water. This way, there will be enough water for next week.

It has been a busy day. The Lees liked working at the snack stand. They would like to work at the stand again soon.

Now it is time to go home. Mr. Lee locks the snack stand. The Lees agree. Game day was fun!

Glossary

add to join 2 groups

divide to place into equal groups

multiply to join equal groups

subtract to take away objects from a group or to compare groups

volunteer a person who does a job without getting paid